THE

SEVEN WONDERS

OF

NEW JERSEY

—and then some

by

Thomas C. Murray
and
Valerie Barnes

ENSLOW PUBLISHERS
Bloy Street and Ramsey Avenue
Box 777
Hillside, New Jersey 07205

The authors wish to thank Charles F. Cummings, Supervising Librarian, New Jersey Reference Division, Newark Public Library, for reviewing the manuscript, and Karen Diane Gilbert, of the same division, for preparing the index.

974.9
Mur

Library of Congress Cataloging in Publication Data:

Murray, Thomas Christopher, 1933-
    The seven wonders of New Jersey—and then some.

    SUMMARY: Presents a brief history, description, and other pertinent information about 14 natural and 14 man-made wonders in New Jersey.
    1. New Jersey—Miscellanea. 2. Curiosities and wonders—New Jersey. [1. New Jersey—Miscellanea. 2. New Jersey—Description and travel—Guides. 3. Curiosities and wonders] I. Barnes, Valerie, joint author. III. Title.

F134.M87   974.9   80-16424
ISBN 0-89490-016-1
ISBN 0-89490-017-X (pbk.)

Printed in the United States of America

10   9   8   7   6   5   4   3   2   1

Contents

Foreword

New Jersey, although one of the nation's smallest states, is a land of vivid contrasts. There are mountains and beaches, lakes and forests, fertile farmlands and vast stretches of pine stands.

Historically, New Jersey shares its roots with the earliest colonies on the Atlantic Seaboard. It was one of the original thirteen states, and because of its location, became the "cockpit" of the American Revolution. The expansion of the United States was reflected in the state's successive canal-, railroad-, and turnpike-building eras and in the burgeoning factories and cities. New Jersey slid into the twentieth century on a wave of progressivism and reform, and today it is a "little giant" with its vast resources in industry and finance, its green lands and transportation systems, and the rich diversity of its people.

New Jersey is a great state—with its changing landscape and more than 350-year-old legacy from the past. Some 20,000 teenagers also decided it was a wonder-filled state, when they selected the Seven-plus-Seven Wonders of New Jersey.

Students in the Jerseymen History Clubs, the youth branch of The New Jersey Historical Society, selected 28 candidates for the Wonders of New Jersey. In classrooms and in school assemblies, thousands debated the attractions. Ballots were distributed, and the seven most popular natural and man-made sites were voted the Wonders of the state.

The enthusiasm of students, adults, and the media was one of the most pleasant dividends of the "Wonders search." Schools in south Jersey inquired about directions to the Delaware Water Gap and the Great Falls of Passaic. Those in the northern section requested pictures of Lucy, the Margate Elephant. All areas were justly proud of the 127 miles of beaches and shoreline.

Radio, television, and newspapers acclaimed New Jersey's natural and man-made attractions. They discovered in the list a popular site for almost everyone throughout the state. As important, they gave wide coverage to Jerseyans taking a justifiable pride in their homeland.

The final roster of wonders may still be debatable. Many grass-roots favorites were overlooked but still remain local marvels to towns and counties. Almost anyone who knows and loves New Jersey will have a dark-horse favorite not included in this volume.

We hope so, as this underlines the evidence that this complex, robust little state is abundantly filled with wonders.

Joan C. Hull
Executive Director
The New Jersey Historical Society

Introduction

The seven natural wonders and seven man-made wonders of New Jersey were selected from nominations by the Jerseymen clubs in 90 secondary schools throughout the state. The Jerseymen, sponsored by The New Jersey Historical Society, compiled a list of 14 natural wonders and 14 man-made wonders. The list then was voted on by more than 20,000 students to decide the top seven in each category. The remaining nominations in each category have been included in this book also as "runners-up" wonders.

The project was originated by Thomas C. Murray, who is a teacher of social studies at Mater Dei High School in New Monmouth, New Jersey. The Jerseymen club of Mater Dei High School, along with the New Jersey Historical Society, co-sponsored the Wonders Search.

Lists of the biggest, the best, the most, and so on, have been compiled for centuries. One of the most famous is the *Seven*

Wonders of the Ancient World. It was compiled in the second century B.C. by Antipater of Sidon by culling ancient guide-books. His wonders were:

> The pyramids of Egypt
> The gardens of Semiramis at Babylon
> The statue of Zeus at Olympia
> The temple of Artemis at Ephesus
> The Mausoleum at Halicarnassus
> The Colossus at Rhodes
> The Pharos (lighthouse) of Alexandria

Why seven? In the sixth century B.C. Pythagoras, a Greek philosopher and mathematician, maintained that the number seven was associated with sacred things.

The wonders of the ancient world were all man-made, but extensive interest in nature sent people traveling in the late eighteenth century, and the outstanding beauties of nature were compiled in a list of the Seven Natural Wonders of the World.* This list comprised:

> The Grand Canyon, Colorado River, Arizona
> The Rio de Janeiro harbor
> The Iguassu Falls, Argentina
> The Yosemite Valley and the Giant Sequoias of
>   California
> Mt. Everest, on the border of Tibet and Nepal
> The Nile River, Egypt
> The Northern Lights (aurora borealis)

New Jersey may not have a Grand Canyon, but it does have wonderful places to learn about and visit.

---

* *This list appeared in Collier's Encyclopedia.*

PART
I

NATURAL
WONDERS

1

Delaware Water Gap

The Delaware Water Gap, the spectacular natural wonder in the rugged mountain country of the northwest corner of New Jersey, is a phenomenon of millions of years of extremes of weather and the wrenching and twisting of the earth's crust. The mighty Delaware River, through the millenia, cut downward through the quartzite rock of the Kittatinny Mountains as they rose, resulting in a 150-foot wide Delaware River bed flanked by the towering, wrinkled, and squeezed rock lifts of the Kittatinnies, a part of the Appalachian chain exhibiting a wild, uninhabited beauty. The continuation of this mountain range in Pennsylvania is called the Blue Mountain and in New York, the Shawungunk.

For more than a century, the Delaware Water Gap has been a lure to visitors because of its awe-inspiring natural beauty. The attractions are the invigorating mountain air, the panoramic view, and the undisturbed beauty away from the bustle and noise of the metropolis.

The view from the craggy crest is a kaleidoscope: meticulously-maintained farmlands seemingly bound together with a jigsaw pattern of twisting country roads; the majestic Delaware inching eternally to the sea; in the summer, clusters of mountain laurel painting the landscape; and in the winter, a thick frosting of ice giving the vertical walls the aura of an oddly misplaced iceberg awaiting the spring thaw for an escape to the open sea.

Unlike the iceberg or the fleeting color of laurel, however, the grandeur of the Gap will be permanent. The Delaware Water Gap National Recreation Area was authorized by Congress in 1965 to preserve more than 70,000 unspoiled acres along the river boundary of New Jersey and Pennsylvania. Part of the plan called for construction of a dam at Tocks Island to create a 37-mile-long lake in the Delaware. This reservoir was designed to provide water for the tri-state area and to assist in flood control.

The plan was bitterly fought by conservationists who believed it would destroy the beauty of the Delaware River. The conservationists won.

The U.S. Department of the Interior is proposing to expand the park facilities to provide outdoor recreation for nearly three million visitors a year. A large part of the development is to include the site once slated for the Tocks Island dam.

The attractions now include three beaches on the river bank and at a lake, campsites, hiking trails, picnic areas, and areas for sailing and canoeing. In the winter, a ski trail, ice-skating, and ice-fishing are enjoyed, and a snowmobile trail is provided.

Park rangers offer environmental education programs in such topics as agriculture, pollution control, and archaeology. There are museums, on-site exhibitions and a campfire program; and a small community of skilled artisans and craftsmen works at Peters Valley Craft Village in the National Recreation Area just north of the Gap.

American landscape painters, including such noted artists as Carl Bodmer and George Inness, have been capturing the area's beauty on canvas since the 1800s. Today, artists and art students work under an "Artists for Environment" program sponsored by the National Park Service at Wallpack Center near the Gap.

For those with imagination, there is a challenge to discover the giant profile of an Indian formed by the craggy rocks atop Mt. Tammany a short distance from the Kittatinny Overlook.

Delaware Water Gap
(United States Department of the Interior, National Park Service)

INFORMATION: National Park Service, Delaware Water Gap National Park, Bushkill, PA 18324. (717) 588-6637. Open daily except Christmas. Tours of Peters Valley Craft Village are conducted daily except Mondays, and tickets are available at the nearby country store.

DIRECTIONS: Route 80 west to the Delaware River. Marked roadways lead to the Information Center.

2

Great Falls
of the Passaic River

The Great Falls of the Passaic River is a natural wonder set in
the midst of a man-made wonder, the historic industrial center
of Paterson, New Jersey's third largest city. About a billion
gallons of water flow over the 77-foot-high falls each day. This
water was harnessed to make America's first planned industrial
city. You can read more about this old city in the chapter on
Society for Establishing Useful Manufactures (S.U.M.).

The Great Falls is located where the Passaic River crosses
the first ridge of the Watchung Mountains. Almost 200 million
years ago, when the great dinosaurs roamed the land, an underground disturbance pushed molten rock up through the earth's
surface. Most of this heat-formed rock, called basalt, makes up
the chasm and cliffs in the falls area. During the last ice age the
Passaic River cut its way through the rock to form its present
course. Over the years, outside forces such as erosion shaped the
present-day Great Falls.

Historical accounts of the falls date back to 1680 when
Dutch missionaries described it "as a sight to be seen in order
to observe the power and wonder of God." Presidents from

George Washington to Gerald Ford visited the falls and marvelled at its splendor. Poets from Washington Irving to William Carlos Williams have echoed the song of the falls. And it was in the waters near the falls that John Holland, an immigrant from Ireland, developed and tested the world's first successful modern submarine.

The use of water from the falls to provide power that turned machines dates to Revolutionary War days, when Alexander Hamilton first realized the falls' potential as an energy source. It was mainly through Hamilton's efforts when he was Secretary of the Treasury, that the Society for Establishing Useful Manufactures (S.U.M.) was established in 1791 (See section on S.U.M.). To make S.U.M. work, a system of man-made channels called raceways was built to bring water from above the falls. As the water rushed downhill through the zigzagging course of raceways, it provided the power necessary to operate the mills along its route.

In 1914, the water energy of the falls was harnessed for use in a hydroelectric power-generating station. The station, which was at the base of the falls, was used until 1969. There are plans to reactivate the hydroelectric station in the near future.

The Great Falls, in its heyday, was as popular a tourist attraction as Niagara Falls is today. It was hailed in guidebooks as one of America's wonders and a "must" for all sightseers. In the 1820s, the falls became so popular that Timothy Crane built the "Cottage on the Cliffs" there. The cottage was complete with guest accomodations, a pavilion for dancing, and the first bridge ever built over the chasm. By the mid-nineteenth century when it became easier to travel long distances, the Great Falls' popularity as a natural wonder was replaced by that of the even more spectacular 167-foot falls of the Niagara River.

Approximately 10,000 tourists visit the Great Falls of the Passaic annually, and it has never lost its attraction for daredevils. The first was Sam Patch, a laborer in a cotton mill. In September,

1827, Patch decided to "jump" the falls. Sam plummeted from the top of the cascade 77 feet to the basin of the falls below. To the amazement of onlookers—and probably himself—Sam survived the leap. He later jumped Niagara Falls, but died trying the same stunt at falls on the Genesee River, New York, in 1829. In recent years, spectators have thrilled to other spectacular feats—including a high-wire aerial act by the famous circus family, The Flying Wallendas—and of Philippe Petit, who gained fame for walking a tightrope between the twin towers of New York's 110-story World Trade Center.

The Great Falls Festival is an annual event held during Labor Day Weekend.

INFORMATION: Grace M. George, Great Falls Tours, 80 McBride Ave., Paterson, NJ 07501. (201) 881-3896.

DIRECTIONS: Route 80 east to Paterson Central Business District exit. Left at Grand St., right at Spruce St., right to Haines Overlook Park parking lot.
Route 80 west to Paterson Main St. exit. Left on Grand St., right on Spruce St., right to Haines Overlook Park parking lot.
Garden State Parkway north to Exit 155P, left at Grand St., right on Spruce St., right to Haines Overlook Park parking lot.
Garden State Parkway south to Route 80 west exit. Take Paterson Main St. exit. Left on Grand Street, right on Spruce St., right to Haines Overlook Park parking lot.

Great Falls
(Newark Public Library Photo)

3

High Point State Park

High Point State Park is, as its name implies, the highest point in New Jersey.

People refer to New Jersey's tallest mountains as "hills," but High Point reaches a perfectly respectable 1803 feet above sea level.

The park area of 13,019 acres of rare, unspoiled forest north of the town of Sussex, is in the extreme northwest corner of the state, lying along the crest of the Kittatinny Mountains. It was a gift of the state, in 1923, from Colonel and Mrs. Anthony R. Kuser of Bernardsville. Colonel Kuser was a renowned naturalist with a lifelong interest in birds. He wanted the area to remain in its natural state.

Dominating the summit is a 220-foot-tall granite obelisk, a memorial dedicated to New Jersey's war heroes.

From High Point one can see the farms of the Delaware Valley and the Pocono ridges to the west. In the valley far below lies Port Jervis, New York, where Tri-State Rock marks the point at which Pennsylvania, New York, and New Jersey meet at the confluence of the Neversink and Delaware Rivers.

Looking northeast one sees the Catskill Mountains, and to the south lie the neat farms and woodlands of Sussex County. More than 60 miles south are the Kittatinny Ridge and the Delaware Water Gap, which can be seen on a clear day.

The cool water of spring-fed Lake Marcia invites swimmers. The Appalachian Trail runs through High Point State Park and the adjacent Stokes State Forest. Parking areas, bathhouses, and refreshments are nearby.

Twenty-acre Sawmill Lake, three miles south of the obelisk, provides privacy and peace for campers. There is a bathing beach, and each campsite has tables and benches.

Picnicking is pleasant, with fireplaces, water, and comfort stations nearby. Shelters protect visitors in rainy weather. Some picnic areas are designed for use by large groups.

Fishing for trout and bass is permitted, as are small non-powered boats. Hunting is prohibited. A number of rustic cabins along the shore of Steenykill Lake are available from May to October.

If you stand on a rocky ridge in autumn, you may see some of the thousands of hawks, with outstretched wings, heading southward for the winter. The westerly winds strike the flanks of the long ridges and create a strong updraft that enables the birds to glide effortlessly. They seldom have to flap their wings. Thousands of Canada Geese, as well as warblers and other small birds, also migrate along the ridge.

Throughout the state park, trails are marked to direct hikers to the various areas of scenic beauty and recreation.

The park is open for winter sports also, such as ice-skating, sledding, ice fishing, cross-country skiing, and snowmobiling.

The Dryden Kuser Natural Area, at Cedar Swamp, north of High Point, named for the donors' son, is used for scientific and educational studies. Cedar Swamp is an area of virgin woodland, with tall hemlock, white pine, black spruce, white cedar, red maple, and a great variety of plants. Here one can see unique combinations of white and red cedar growing side-by-side.

Colonel Kuser's 30-room residence, "The Lodge," with its spectacular tri-state views from the veranda, is maintained by the state Department of Environmental Protection, but has been closed to the public for two years. Members of a local historical society have been studying suitable uses for the building.

High Point State Park
(Newark Public Library Photo)

INFORMATION: High Point State Park, R.R.4, Box 287, Sussex, NJ 07461. (201) 875-4800. Open daily, year-round, depending on weather conditions. Fees are collected Memorial Day through Labor Day. The fees are $1.00 Mondays, Wednesdays, Thursdays, and Fridays. Saturdays and Sundays and holidays the fee is $3.00. No fee on Tuesdays. Monument admission is twenty-five cents, collected on weekends in May and in October.

DIRECTIONS: Route 23 north to High Point State Park.

4

New Jersey Shoreline

The New Jersey shore is everything under the sun. It is New Jersey's most precious natural resource.

Visitors can bask in the sun on the shore's 127 miles of sandy beaches and inlets from Sandy Hook to the tip of Cape May.

The shore is vanishing footprints in the sand, saltwater taffy, sand castles, advertising streamers trailing low-flying airplanes, and the Miss America Pageant.

The shore is marble tournaments, kite festivals, baby parades, and children searching for seashells.

The shore also is fishing in Belmar, climbing up in the Old Barney lighthouse, and sailing on the Navesink. There are man-made attractions: the boardwalk arcades at Seaside Heights, Asbury Park, and Wildwood, and the bustling casino life at Atlantic City. For natural surroundings and solitude, there are Brigantine, Stone Harbor, and Avalon.

Eight presidents have enjoyed the sea breezes at Long Branch. Quiet orderliness and small-town appeal are found at Ocean Grove, a community that grew out of a Methodist camp meeting in 1869.

Comfortable old Victorian homes with wicker rocking chairs on the verandas are found at Rumson, Deal, Bay Head, and Cape May, contrasting with row upon row of summer beach cottages.

The shore is a network of fiercely independent towns protecting their stretches of ocean and their images.

The shore is ever-changing. Hurricanes and storms have battered its coastline. The never-ending tides continue their perpetual shifting of the sands.

Tourism has been the major shore industry since visitors first arrived on horseback in the eighteenth century. Later, vacationers took the train, or came by bus or even boat. The Garden State Parkway, completed from Cape May to Paramus in July, 1955, made the shore more accessible.

The shore has experienced difficult environmental problems: sludge, nuclear power plants, and visual reminders of over-development. Another serious problem is erosion, as the tides nibble away constantly at the shifting sands.

Atlantic City, "Queen of all seaside resorts," is a magnet year-round, with its hotels, both early twentieth century and ultra modern, its casinos, and its convention appeal. It is famous for its boardwalk and as the site of the Miss America Pageant, a September tradition.

There is the charm of Long Beach Island, an 18-mile strip of low and high dunes, and Loveladies, an art colony of some reputation.

The New Jersey shore has been attracting treasure hunters for centuries. Historians estimate as many as 500 ships wrecked off the coast, and tales of Captain Kidd and buried treasure at Sandy Hook continue to fascinate new visitors. Tourists delight in discovering Cape May "diamonds," semi-precious pebbles that sometimes wash up on the sand.

The widest New Jersey beaches are on the southern islands. One of the broadest along the Atlantic coast is at Wildwood. At low tide, you can wade out nearly one-fourth of a mile to search for sand dollars, conch shells, starfish, or sea horses.

Many of the shore's lighthouses survive as stark sentinels from the past. They can be seen at Barnegat Light, Cape May Point, Sandy Hook, and Absecon.

Fishing villages can be found from Sea Bright southward to Cape May, reminders of a prosperous whaling industry in early Cape May. Sports fishing continues as a flourishing business.

From the Highlands south there is some of the best off-shore fishing on the East Coast. Sportsmen can choose from among hundreds of charter and party boats in Highlands, Point Pleasant, Brielle, Toms River, Barnegat, Forked River, Atlantic City, Sea Isle City, Avalon, and Wildwood.

Depending on the season, there's fishing for flounder, whiting, cod, mackerel, bluefish, striped bass, porgy, sea bass, fluke, and tuna. There is also excellent fishing from the jetties, piers, and bridges along the shore.

No place in New Jersey is far from the coastline.

New Jersey Shoreline
(Bureau of Parks)

INFORMATION: Department of Environmental Protection, Division of Coastal Resources, P. O. Box 1889, Trenton, NJ 08625. "A Guide to New Jersey Beaches" contains listings of beach facilities, activites, and special events in 46 shore communities. Beach/Fishing Telephone Reports is a weekly report on the condition of the beaches as well as salt and fresh water fishing. Call (609) 292-8277.

DIRECTIONS: From northern New Jersey, major east-west roads are Routes 80, 46, 287, connecting with the Garden State Parkway south which has marked exits at many shore points. Toll-free Route 9 parallels the Parkway. From the Trenton area take Route 195 to the end. Follow signs to Lakewood, then east to Parkway.
From the Philadelphia area Route 70 and the Atlantic City Expressway toll road lead to the shore.

5

℘Palisades

The spectacular Palisades, dominating the west bank of the Hudson River in Hudson and Bergen counties, was appropriately named for the type of fortification it resembles—a row of long stakes set closely together.

The columnar face of the Palisades was created millions of years ago when molten lava from the underlying sandstone boiled through the cracks in the rocks, expanding them. Upon cooling, the rocks contracted into a long row of vertical columns, as if designed by an early Greek or Roman sculptor, and as high as 50-foot skyscrapers.

The Palisades is best viewed from the east on a crisply-clear morning when the sun, rising over the horizon, casts a rosy glow on the stark, towering, rock formation, emphasizing the perpendicular crevices between the columns.

The unique cliffs, which so enthralled Henry Hudson and his Half Moon crew when they sailed up the Hudson River in 1609, appeared doomed for a number of years late last century when quarry crews began to strip away the cliffside to provide paving blocks for construction of New York streets.

The despoliation outraged the women of New Jersey and, in 1896, 300 members of the State Federation of Women's Clubs marched on Trenton to protest. Lobbyists for the quarrymen were just as active, but in 1900, the women were successful, and the Palisades Interstate Park Commission was created to save the Palisades for posterity.

The Palisades formation extends northward into New York State. The Palisades section of the Interstate Park is more than twelve miles long and includes more than 2,500 acres. It extends from just south of the George Washington Bridge, in Edgewater, to about a half mile over the New York line. The Commission is an example of cooperation between New Jersey and New York to benefit all of us.

Its commanding view of the Hudson River made the cliff a strategic point in the Revolutionary War, and military control over it changed hands on several occasions.

The view of the Palisades from the east is spectacular, but the panorama from atop the sheer cliff is even more so. The toll-free Palisades Interstate Parkway offers three lookouts for breathtaking views: the Rockefeller Lookout where one can see the New York City skyline; the Alpine Lookout for a view over Yonkers and the rest of Westchester County, and the State Line Lookout for a vista up the northern Hudson past the picturesque Tappan Zee Bridge.

Today, the Palisades provides areas for hiking, picinics, climbing, and cliff exploring from heights of 300 to 530 feet.

Palisades
(Palisades Interstate Park)

INFORMATION: Palisades Park Commission, P.O. Box 155, Alpine, NJ 07620. (201) 768-1360.

DIRECTIONS: In New Jersey the Palisades can be reached from Route 9W and Palisades Interstate Parkway connection from U.S. Route I-95/Route 1 near the George Washington Bridge in Fort Lee. Exit 1 off the Palisades Interstate Parkway leads to Palisades Ave. in Englewood Cliffs —a hairpin-curve drive to the Englewood Boat Basin. Exit 2, to Alpine, is the site of General Cornwallis' headquarters when he ferried his army of 5,000 across the Hudson in mid-winter to attack Fort Lee. Exit 3 leads to the State Line Lookout.

6

Pine Barrens

The Pine Barrens is the largest section of unspoiled vegetation on the East Coast. Its undeveloped acreage covers 2,000 square miles and spills into seven counties, about one-fourth of the state. This unique area of wild woods, cranberries, and blueberries is also the largest source of pure water in the United States.

Governor Brendan T. Byrne has asked for federal money to purchase the land so it can be held in its unspoiled condition. The state already has purchased 50,000 acres of the most pristine, most threatened land for $12 million.

In the central area of the Pine Barrens is a forest wilderness, an area nearly as large as Yosemite National Park. A few small communities dot the vast acreage in the level land. This land has attracted attention for more than 300 years because of its curious wild beauty.

One of the early industries was lumbering, with loggers clearing the pine and cedar for shipment to shipyards.

Bog iron was discovered here, and forges and furnaces that prospered for a number of decades were built along the streams.

Where the ironworks once stood there are now crumbling ghost towns. Clues are subtle, and it often takes hard looking, detective work, and imagination to reconstruct mentally the long-forgotten settlements.

One of the most important early iron communities was Batsto. The core of this community has remained protected as an authentic early Pine Barrens village. Visitors can see the manor house, workers' cottages, the general store, and the post office.

A visit to Batsto also provides an excellent opportunity for the tourist to hike through part of the famous Pine Barrens on nature trails.

The vast Pine Barrens is alive from late March to early November with more than 400 varieties of wildflowers, wold orchids, water lilies, turkey beard, insect-eating pitcher plants, and the internationally famous curly-leaf ferns. Springtime brings the wild laurel, the summer brings wild orchids and blueberry bushes, and in winter, the long-needled pines are silhouetted against the snow.

Hikers, canoeists, fishermen, naturalists, and those who seek solitude can all find their places in the Pine Barrens.

Some names give clues to the settlers' humor or satire: Mt. Misery; Quaker Bridge, site of a nineteenth century tavern; Apple Pie Hill; and Double Trouble.

Chatsworth in Woodland Township is the principal community in the Pine Barrens, a tiny town of fewer than 100 homes, a post office, a general store, a firehouse, a church, and a school.

Within the Pine Barrens is Wharton State Forest, covering 150 square miles and comprising the largest amount of state-owned forestland in New Jersey. There are picnicking and swimming at Atsion Lake, sites for camping and fishing, and 60 miles of streams for canoe trips.

Also within the Pine Barrens are Lebanon State Forest, Bass River State Forest, Penn State Forest, and Belleplain State

Forest. These are woodlands   dedicated to forest research, recreation, and timber production.

Federal lands near the fringes of the Pine Barrens are Fort Dix and its neighbor, McGuire Air Force Base. Fort Dix served as an army training center during World War I. McGuire, established 20 years later, includes 36,000 acres. McGuire is dedicated to providing strategic airlift to other branches of the service. The McGuire community includes about 10,000 military and civilian personnel.

The Pine Barrens offers some of the most beautiful wilderness canoeing in the country. The four rivers in the southern part of the Pine Barrens, the Mullica, the Batsto, the Oswego, and the Wading are the most easily canoed and the most popular.

INFORMATION: Batsto, R.D. 1, Hammonton, NJ 08037. (609) 561-3232. Tours daily from the Batsto Visitor Center from 9 a.m. to 4 p.m. in April, May, June, September, and October. Limited to 20 persons and may be arranged in advance. The grounds are open all year during daylight hours. Buildings may be toured from Memorial Day to Labor Day from 10 a.m. to 6 p.m. For the balance of the year, weekdays 11 a.m. to 5 p.m.; Saturdays, Sundays, and holidays from 11 a.m. to 5 p.m. Frequency of tours depends on availability of guides. The fee is $1. John McPhee's *The Pine Barrens* is considered one of the best books about the region. His portrait of the land and its people is a blend of folklore and the natural resources there.

DIRECTIONS: The Pine Barrens and Batsto may be reached from Route 206 south, to Route 30 south, to 542 east, or the Garden State Parkway and Route 9, south to New Gretna, west on Route 542.

Pine Barrens
(Patricia J. Baxter, New Jersey Conservation Foundation)

7

Sunfish Pond

To many, Sunfish Pond is the last Walden Pond in New Jersey. It is a crystal-clear, half-mile-long pond in Worthington State Forest in Pahaquarry Township. Preservation of the pond in its rare, natural state is a victory for conservationists who campaigned throughout the 1960s to save it for coming generations. The state had sold the pond to two utility companies for use as a pumped-storage reservoir for generating electrical power.

The New Jersey Audubon Society, one of the first organizations to join with the Lenni Lenape League in the fight to save the Sunfish Pond area, described the pond as being "cradled like a precious sapphire in an ice-scoured glacial basin atop the Kittatinny Mountains of the Appalachian Highlands, the oldest mountain range in the world." The society said that Sunfish Pond "personifies the unspoiled natural beauty of America," and they have called it "one of the most scenic treasures of New Jersey."

The rallying cry of the conservationists, led by the Lenni Lenape League and Casey Kays, was "Save Sunfish Pond."

Everywhere the slogan appeared on bumper stickers and T-shirts. Annual hikes to the pond in May attracted more and more attention, and during 1967, it attracted the help of the late Supreme Court Justice William O. Douglas, who brought national recognition to the cause. Until then, even in New Jersey, only a few had heard of the pond, but then the battle drew supporters from all over the state.

The New Jersey Legislature heeded the public outcry and bought back Sunfish Pond, pledging to retain it in its wilderness state.

Until the utility companies "discovered" Sunfish, only a relatively few hardy naturalists were familiar with it because it is accessible only by a strenuous uphill hike on the Appalachian Trail.

The 41-acre Sunfish Pond is located at the crest of Kittatinny Ridge. It is a completely natural lake in the ridge, its basin scoured out by the irresistible force of glaciers of the last ice age. It is a geologic rarity.

In April, 1970, the Department of the Interior announced that Sunfish Pond had been approved for inclusion in the National Registry of Natural Landmarks. The landmark area comprises 188 acres.

In May, 1973, a native-stone monument, bearing a bronze plaque noting that the pond is a registered landmark, was erected. The monument is located along the Appalachian Trail about 150 feet from the southwestern end of the pond.

All camping, swimming, boating, and fires are prohibited in order to preserve the pond, trees, stone paths, and rare plants found near the pond. Surrounding Sunfish Pond is a forest that is home to foxes, rabbits, pheasant, and to one of the largest deer herds in the state.

Sunfish Pond
(Bureau of Parks)

INFORMATION: The National Park Service, Route 80, Columbia, NJ 07832. (201) 496-4458. Open every day except Christmas. The staff provides full information and maps of the area.

DIRECTIONS: Kittatinny Point Information Station in the Delaware Water Gap National Recreation Area. The Recreation Area is clearly marked by signs off Route 80 along the Delaware River. From the headquarters Sunfish Pond is a strenuous 3.75-mile hike each way along the Appalachian Trail.

8

Franklin Mineral Deposits

The discovery of zinc ore in the iron deposits in Franklin started a new industry for New Jersey, and in 1848, the Franklin mine initiated the nation's zinc output.

Zinc oxide for use as a paint additive was , for many years, the principal product of the Franklin mine. The New Jersey Zinc Company worked the mine at Franklin until the ore ran out in 1954. Since then the mine has been a mecca for mineral and rock collectors.

Dr. Samuel Fowler developed the deposits at Franklin, called the ore Franklinite, and formulated the oxide that was used as a paint base.

Today, a replica of the huge mine is an attraction in Sussex County, and the relics of the mining industry are on display at the mineral museum. Visitors can enter the working replica of the famous Franklin mine, as it was 18 levels below the ground. This mine replica is a project of the Kiwanis Club of Franklin. More than 300 specimens of rock may be seen in the fluorescent room, where many of the minerals glow in a wide variety of colors under ultraviolet lights. The town of Franklin calls itself "The Fluorescent Mineral Capital of the World."

Franklin is noted for its minerals the world over, and 280 different minerals have been found at the site, including many never found elsewhere, and many yet to be classified.

For many science classes at schools and colleges and for individual geologists and rock hounds a visit to Franklin is a "must."

After touring the museum, they head for the old zinc-mine rock dump, called the Buckwheat Dump, where they can search for mineral specimens. A mineral show is held early in October.

Franklin has not forgotten the miners. Outside the museum stands a life-size bronze figure of a miner with his hard hat and miner's carbide lamp, a reminder of the many thousands who worked the Franklin mines for 106 years.

Deposits of iron and zinc ore still are present in scattered areas of the New Jersey highlands even though mining has been phased out. Strata vary from a few inches to as much as 50 feet or more in thickness, with an average of four to 20 feet.

The town of Franklin turned over to the museum the administration of the Buckwheat Dump. The museum is continually acquiring new specimens of superior grade so visitors will always be able to study the best of Franklin's minerals. The museum has its own laboratory for the identification and preparation of minerals to be displayed.

N.J. Zinc Co. in Franklin
(Newark Public Library Photo)

INFORMATION: Franklin Museum, Inc., Box 76, 6-B Evans St., Franklin, NJ 07416 (Sussex County). (201) 827-3481. In July and August the museum is open Wednesday through Sunday from 10 a.m. to 4:30 p.m. (Dump closes at 4 p.m.). Open by appointment Tuesday, Wednesday, and Thursday, April 15 to November 15. Open Friday and Saturday 10 a.m. to 4 p.m., Sunday 12:30 p.m. to 4 p.m. Admission fee is $1.50 for adults; seventy-five cents for high school students; fifty cents for grammar school students. There is an additional fee of $1.50 for adults, fifty cents for grammar school students, and seventy-five cents for high school students for admission to the Dump.

DIRECTIONS: Take Route 23 north, Route 206 north, or Route 15 north to Route 94, east to Hamburg and Route 23 south to Franklin (Sussex County).

9

Great Swamp
National Wildlife Refuge

The Great Swamp, just south of Morristown, is a microcosm of nature with its 6,500 acres of swamps, hardwood forests, and marshlands, as well as open fields and lowlands.

The swamp was formed more than 15,000 years ago by glacial action on the earth's crust. When the melting Wisconsin glacier receded slowly across the Passaic Valley, it left behind ancient Lake Passaic, which drained into the Passaic River. The Great Swamp is the marshy bed of the former lake.

It took a group of dedicated Morris County residents and nine years to save the swamp and surrounding wilderness from conversion into a 10,000-acre jetport proposed by the Port Authority of New York and New Jersey.

Conservationists and almost 15,000 individuals contributed time and money, and almost 500 organizations were active in saving the swamp.

The battle against the Port Authority ended when, in 1968, the Great Swamp was classified as a national wilderness area. It was a landmark event.

The refuge's wildlife observation center and the Morris

County Education Center both have boardwalks for wilderness walks, and a number of primitive trails are available.

Some 250,000 visitors tour the Great Swamp National Wildlife Refuge every year. The swamp is open dawn to dusk throughout the year; however, the best times to visit are in spring and fall.

The first flower to show in the spring is the skunk cabbage unfurling its big leaves. Redwing blackbirds nest among marsh cattails, golden marsh marigolds, cinnamon ferns, and a wealth of other green plants.

In autumn, long after the swamp maples have dropped their flaming leaves, the witch hazel unrolls its tiny blossoms, the last flower of the year. Sun shimmers through the bare branches of old gray birches.

The swamps, fresh-water marshes, bogs, and uplands produce a rich diversity of wildlife. More than 200 species of birds can be seen. Wood ducks thrive and more than 4,000 ducklings are hatched each year in the refuge. Interesting drop-ins include goshawks, ospreys, and eagles, since the refuge is along their migration path.

White tail deer, muskrat, fox, and mink make their homes in the swamp. Sometimes otter and beaver appear. The rare blue-spotted salamander and bog turtle also are at home here.

Botanical species include fern mosses, wild lilies, orchids, primroses, marigolds, and gentians.

For a visit it is best to take waterproof footwear for off-boardwalk hikes, especially in the wilderness area. Insect repellent in the summer is a good idea.

Great Swamp National Wildlife Refuge
(Valerie Barnes)

INFORMATION: Great Swamp National Wildlife Refuge, R.F.D., Box 148, Basking Ridge, NJ 07920. (201) 647-1222. Open every day of the year from 8 a.m. until dark. Groups may arrange in advance for a film and lecture in the headquarters auditorium. There are special education programs on weekdays. A self-guide tour and map are available at the information office. Pets are not allowed and there is no picnic area. The Outdoor Education Center, operated by the Morris County Park Commission, offers tours for classes (201) 635-6629.

DIRECTIONS: From Route 287 south take the exit marked North Maple Ave., Basking Ridge. Continue right to North Maple Ave., At the yellow blinker light turn left onto Madisonville Rd. When you cross the bridge, the road becomes Lee's Hill Rd. Continue for about two miles. Just before the Harding Township School turn right onto Long Hill Rd. and follow it to the parking lot.

10

Hackensack Meadowlands

The Hackensack Meadowlands is a 20,000-acre tract which contains nearly 5,000 acres of tidal-flowed lands, woodlands, marshes, and meadows. It is larger than Manhattan Island, 20 times as large as Central Park, and is the heart of the world's most densely populated urban complex.

The area's natural history began as the last glacier retreated— 20,000 to 40,000 years ago, geologists believe. Melting ice formed glacial Lake Hackensack reaching from Perth Amboy almost to Haverstraw, New York.

The ancient lake eventually drained into the ocean, leaving behind the Hackensack River, which meets the ocean tides of Newark Bay at the Meadowlands we know today.

The highways and railroad tracks now crossing the Meadowlands began as Indian footpaths and cedar-plank roads built by settlers in the area's early history. Nature's whims and the lack of proper technology caused early attempts to block the flooding tidal waters and produce farm land to fail. The swamp became a dumping ground.

In 1959 the New Jersey Department of Conservation and Economic Development began the campaign for rehabilitation of this remarkable land. In 1968 the legislature authorized the

Hackensack Meadowlands Development Commission to design and administer the Meadowlands for public use. Seventy-five hundred acres were already developed when the HMDC was formed. Today, over half of the land that was still open in 1972 is now set aside for open spaces, marsh preservation for wildfowl use, and water areas for recreation. This open-space network constitutes 6,970 acres.

Efforts to restore the river and wetlands to health are working. Crustaceans, fish, and birds, common before the garbage assault devastated the marshes, are now returning.

The turnabout in environmental quality has been startling. Oil slicks and toxic chemicals once drove all life from the waterways. Fishermen, hunters, and crabbers are now catching legal limits.

The Meadowlands marsh areas show recovery from years of pollution and neglect. The freshwater marsh and adjoining areas are home to a whole community of marsh-dwellers—oysters, mussels, clams, shrimp, crabs, striped bass, and an occasional flounder.

The abundant bird life is seen in the large flocks of ducks, geese, terns, gulls, herons, plovers, sandpipers, and, now and then, a godwit.

Spring and fall evenings bring the passage of countless birds, sometimes obscuring the setting sun as they wing their way on an early nocturnal migration.

The marsh hawk, once an endangered species, has found a home in the Meadowlands. Recently, two breeding pairs were photographed, and chicks have hatched to join the small adult population.

Development and protection were the two goals of the master plan of the Hackensack Meadowlands Development Commission. The plan called for sane and ecologically sound ways of reclaiming land and handling solid waste for 144 communities. It also sought methods of protecting and increasing the existing wildlife and fish population, of protecting the yet unspoiled areas of the district, and of producing 1,000 acres of upland public parks for people to enjoy.

Despite all the development in the Meadowlands since the start of the 1970s, several trappers remain active here. In the 1977-78 season, 32,000 muskrats were trapped in Bergen County, the third highest catch in the state.

Meadowlands planners look forward to a time when the scar of the huge garbage dumps, 50,000 tons of garbage from six counties discarded in the dumps each week, will become a serene expanse providing solitude and recreation for New Jersey metropolitan area residents. It is an enormous project, for the dumps must be shut, and alternate means of disposing of trash must be found.

The 2,000-acre park resulting from the project will be owned by the state. Its major components will be 1,186 acres of now-protected tidal wetlands, bays, creeks, and marshes, known as the Sawmill Creek Wildlife Management Area, and 1,814 acres of upland parks—for field sports, tennis, camping biking, skiing, picnicing, basketball, and jogging.

Sawmill Creek is a delicate estuarial offshoot of the Hackensack River and Newark Bay. Various pollution controls in the last three years have led to a gradual environmental rebirth of the Sawmill Creek preserve. It is emerging once again as a migratory stop for birds on the Atlantic Flyway and as a spawning and nesting ground for fish, waterfowl, and blue-claw crabs.

There now are walkways, horseback riding trails, canoeing in the meandering creeks, wildlife observation towers, and crabbing and hunting stations in the bays and creek.

At intervals, new building projects appear from the meadow, spires rising from meadow grass and cattails.

The Sawmill Creek section of the New Jersey Wildlife Management area includes about 1,186 acres of marshland in southern Lyndhurst, North Arlington, and northern Kearny. A series of trails and boardwalks will offer access to the region, the largest expanse of salt marsh in the Meadowlands.

Hackensack Meadowlands
(Robert C. Grant, HMDC)

INFORMATION: The Hackensack Meadowlands Development Commission, 200 Murray Hill Parkway, East Rutherford, NJ 07073. (201) 460-1700.

DIRECTIONS: From Route 3 take the Lyndhurst Corporate Center exit. Follow Polito Rd. to Valley Brook Ave. Left on Valley Brook Ave. for one mile. By the summer of 1981, this will be the entrance to the Richard De Korte State Park. It is presently the Bergen County landfill. A portion of the 2000-acre Richard De Korte State Park is scheduled to open in the summer of 1981. The 1186-acre Sawmill Creek Wildlife Management Area will be maintained in a natural state. Eight hundred and fourteen acres of former landfill is being transformed into a park. An Environmental Education Center is scheduled to be constructed two miles south of the Sports Complex.

11

New Jersey Bog Iron

Deep in the brandy-colored stream beds of the Pine Barrens, a bog ore can still be found, a variety of the mineral limonite, upon which an entire iron industry was founded in Colonial times.

The Indians made use of the bog ore without knowing what it was. Later, fortunes were made when the demand for iron was created by the French and Indian War and the Revolutionary War.

Bog iron is created by chemical reaction of iron salts in streambeds to decayed vegetable matter. This reaction carries the iron to the surface of the water where it oxidizes. As the deposits pile up, usually mixed with mud, they harden into thick and rocky ore beds. When beds are mined, they yield the substance from which our ancestors obtained their iron. Exhausted ore beds renew themselves in about 20 years.

The bog ores, as their name indicates, are found in bogs and swamps, often immediately under the grass roots, and also in the bottoms of shallow lakes into which swamp waters drain. In New Jersey they are found mainly in the southern portion of the state.

The heart of the pineland ironworks was the furnace that extracted the iron from the bog ore. Usually the rough product was given the form of long bars, or "pigs." Furnaces ran seven days a week, 24 hours a day, shutting down only when the streams froze in winter, halting the waterwheels and machinery.

The munitions boom created by the War of 1812 brought the zenith of the bog-iron industry. Before long, however, the bog-iron deposits began to run low. Either their self-replenishment by nature did not keep up to schedule, or the ore beds were so exploited as to prevent the limonite deposits from accumulating properly in the stream bed. When bog-iron production started in New Jersey, ores seemed abundant, but most deposits were exhausted in less than 50 years.

In 1830 there were fourteen furnaces and the same number of forges mainly dependent upon bog iron for their supply of ore. As early as 1868, however, they were all abandoned. Magnetite had already gained popularity as the cheapest source of iron, and the bog-iron industry succumbed.

The center of the bog-iron industry was the Batsto region, and the closing of the Batsto furnace marked the end of iron production in the Pine Barrens. The bog-iron furnaces, with their 30-foot stacks, were shut down.

Today bog ore has little economic value, and none of the south New Jersey bog-iron furnaces stand.

During the height of the bog-iron industry, James Allaire took over Monmouth furnace, built a town for his more than 500 employees, and opened a school for their children. The ironworks transformed local bog iron into pig iron that was turned into pots, kettles, irons, scissors, stoves, and more. Pig iron was shipped to Allaire's foundry in New York. The village prospered until competition forced the plant to close.

The village became deserted. Now it's alive again. There are more than 3,000 acres to explore.

Allaire Village is a historical restoration of an early

nineteenth century ironworks and workers' village. Visitors can tour the buildings.

Today the Deserted Village of Allaire is a popular attraction for village festivals, antique exhibits, dog shows, and other events.

Historic Batsto (General Store)
(New Jersey Department of Environmental Protection)

INFORMATION: Batsto, R.D. 1 Hammonton, NJ 08037.
(609) 561-3232. Grounds open year-round during daylight
hours. Several buildings may be toured, with a guide, from
Memorial Day to Labor Day, 10 a.m. to 6 p.m. Rest of the
year daily, 11 a.m. to 5 p.m. Fee is $1.00. Tours start at
the Batsto store, 9 a.m. to 4 p.m., April through June and
September and October. The Deserted Village of Allaire,
Box 220, Farmingdale, NJ 07727. (201) 938-2371. Buildings open 10 a.m. to 5 p.m. daily April through October;
weekends only in March. The fee is $2.00 per car, fifty
cents for each person 12 and over.

DIRECTIONS: For Batsto, take Route 206 south from
Trenton, Route US 30 south to Route 542 east or the
Garden State Parkway south and exit at New Gretna,
connecting with Route 542 west. For Allaire State Park
and the Deserted Village of Allaire, take Route 34 south or
the Garden State Parkway to the Spring Lake exit.

12

Ramapo Fault

The Ramapo Fault is an earthquake fracture in the rock strata extending from Peekskill, New York, southwest to Peapack-Gladstone in Somerset County. It is named for the Ramapo Mountains, the New Jersey range of the Hudson Highlands mountain range.

The fault, not visible, was discovered by scientists about 100 years ago. It cuts across Rockland County in New York southward through Mahwah and Oakland in Bergen County into Pompton Lakes in Passaic County and across Morris County into Somerset County.

The most powerful earthquake in New Jersey in 16 years occurred in the fault in July, 1978. Seismologists at the Lamont-Doherty Geological Observatory in Palisades, New York, said the tremor consisted of a main shock and two aftershocks that registered a 3 on the Richter scale.

The Ramapo Fault is active and scientists at the Observatory are studying the relationship between the smaller quakes and the larger ones. On August 10, 1884, an earthquake occurred along the fault that registered 5 on the Richter scale.

The seismologists, who have recorded more than a dozen minor tremors along the fault since 1962, said the earthquake supported a theory that the Ramapo Fault was not inactive, as had been long assumed.

The quakes suggest that the Ramapo Fault may be awakening from its dormant state. The billion-year-old fault was active 200 million years ago but quieted down to such an extent that most scientists have not considered it a site of possible earthquakes.

Some scientists think that the minor earthquakes along the Ramapo Fault are evidence of a build-up of subterranean pressure that will be relieved in a major earthquake someday.

The Ramapo Fault, according to experts at the Observatory, underwent at least four periods of movement from the Precambrian Era, more than 600 million years ago, to the separation of Africa and North America, 150 million years ago. That rupture seemed to reactivate all faults in eastern North America, including the Ramapo—an activity that continues, although considerably diminished.

The Ramapo Fault is an ancient geological fissure similar to but much smaller than the San Andreas Fault in California.

The Lamont scientists began studying the Ramapo Fault closely in 1971, and they have put seismic instruments in the ground throughout the area. Since 1974 about 20 earthquakes ranging in magnitude from 1.5 to 3 have occurred in the fault.

Over the next century scientists say the Ramapo Fault is likely to produce a quake of the intensity that could move trees and shrubs, damage poorly built structures, and crack glassware.

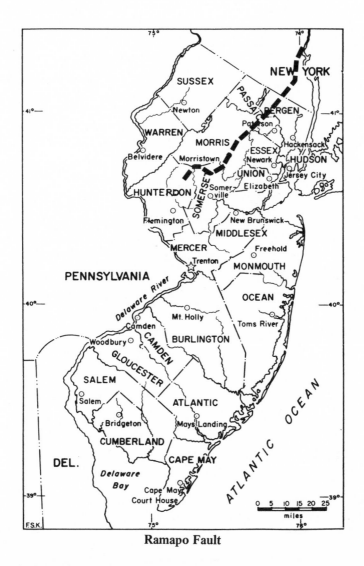

Ramapo Fault

INFORMATION: The Lamont-Doherty Geological Observatory, Palisades, NY 10964. (914) 359-2900. The Observatory holds an open house in October, and visitors can tour and hear a lecture on the work being done.

DIRECTIONS: The Observatory is located off Route 9W, just north of Rockleigh, New Jersey, in Palisades, New York.

13

Roaring Brook

Roaring Brook is a phenomenon of nature that appeals to the ear as much as to the eye. Flowing among and under boulders on its descent down Sourland Mountain in Somerset County, the brook produces a distinctive sound, particularly during spring thaws—a sound that legend says led the early Indians to give the brook its name.

Roaring Brook is a most unusual brook in that in many places it is not visible because it flows below the rocks. The channel width averages 20 to 30 feet and is completely filled with large boulders. The boulders generally are larger halfway up the side of the ridge, 15 to 20 feet long and more than eight feet wide, and the surfaces are weathered. There is no pattern; the long axes may be parallel, perpendicular, or at some angle to the channel direction. Between the boulders are voids often large enough to crawl into, and running water frequently can be seen ten feet or more below the top of the rocks. The channel is free of trees, underbrush, and grass because there is little or no soil.

It is hard to imagine a brook of this size moving such large rocks into its streambed, and there is no evidence that geologic structures such as faults or fracture zones have played a part in the formation of the channel. The probable answer is that if there is a variety of rock sizes and a stream removed all the fine-grained material and small rocks away from the larger boulders, a formation identical to the Roaring Brook channel would be the result.

Because it is in a somewhat deeper valley and it is a permanent stream, Roaring Brook is the only stream to create such an unusual formation. The constant flow of water has been able to remove all but the larger blocks and the deep valley is able to confine flood waters. A smaller intermittent stream may contain water only a few times during the year, and during a flood the erosive force of the water is distributed over a wide area. If a stream is too large, the current might be sufficient to break down and gradually remove even the largest boulders.

Roaring Brook apparently had all the conditions that create such a unique channel.

Some of the unique rock formations are known as The King and Queen's Chair, which resembles two immense armless seats, Table Rock, Devil's Kitchen, and Fort Hans.

Roaring Brook is part of the 1,600 acre Sourland Mountain Preserve to be developed as a passive area by the Somerset County Park Commission.

The preserve began with a donation of 600 acres by the Minnesota Mining and Manufacturing Company, which has an active quarry operation nearby. Additional property has been purchased, and there are plans for multi-use which will offer camping sites and natural areas. The area is now fenced for public safety, and the master plan includes observation platforms over the key features of the brook. Presently there is no timetable for development.

Roaring Brook
(The Somerset County Park Commission)

INFORMATION: Write Somerset County Park Commission, P.O. Box 837, Somerville, NJ 08876. (201) 722-1200. For group tours in limited situations under staff guidance, contact Somerset County Park Commission, 190 Lord Stirling Rd., Basking Ridge, NJ 17920. (201) 766-2489.

DIRECTIONS: From Route 206 at Belle Mead, take Trent Road west at railroad overpass, left on Blawenburg Road one-half mile. At the present there is no public access, and there are limited guided tours only.

14

Tillman Ravine

Tillman Ravine is a picturesque gorge slashing through the southern section of Stokes State Forest. It is easily accessible by a well-used path leading off Brink Road. Steep banks of the ravine are covered with hemlocks and rhododendron and there are, in seasons of high water, fine cascades near its upper end. The hemlocks are kept in an undisturbed state so that the effects of nature can be studied.

Tillman Brook in the gorge creates upper and lower falls.

The area has been set aside as a natural area to be preserved as it was found. To gain a better perspective of the natural features, five bridges have been installed on the lower trail that crosses Tillman Brook.

Hemlocks in Tillman Ravine are as much as four feet in diameter, 112 feet tall, and more than 150 years old.

The source of Tillman Brook is in the side of the Kittatinny Mountains about 1½ miles east. The portion of the stream within Tillman Ravine is in its youthful stages of the river erosion cycle, with a deep narrow valley and steep grade.

A self-guided half-mile circular walking tour from the parking lot can be completed in 45 minutes. After crossing the first wooden bridge, a look downstream shows exposed hemlock roots. A view from the second wooden bridge and a stepping-stone bridge is of rhododendron and the pink flowers of mountain laurel.

Tillman Ravine is a geologic phenomenon formed by stream erosion. The red shale and sandstone rock being eroded is known as the High Falls Formation. This formation was formed about 400 million years ago during the Silurian Period.

Tillman Ravine began to develop about 10,000 years ago. Ice of the last glacier melted away, and small streams started flowing from the spring farther up the ridge. Water flowing down the hill began eroding the rock.

Near the bottom of Tillman Ravine is a structure called the Teacup. This is an example of a pothole, which is formed by swirling sand and rock carried by rapidly-moving water. The swirling motion, much like scouring a pot, deepens and enlarges the pothole, giving it a circular shape and smooth walls. Some of the rocks that helped form the potholes can be seen lying at the bottom.

There are 25 species of deciduous trees to be found as well as red cedar, Eastern hemlock, juniper, Eastern white pine, pitch pine, and red pine.

In June the mountain laurel is in spectacular bloom; in July, the rhododendron; and in September, the witch hazel.

Some of the flowers found here are jack-in-the-pulpit, trout lily, mayapple, meadow buttercup, wild lily of the valley, yellow violets, wild indigo, sheep laurel, Indian pipe, and partridge berry.

Tillman Ravine
(Richard Poots)

INFORMATION: Tillman Ravine, Stokes State Forest, Route 206, Box 260, Branchville, NJ 07826. (201) 948-3820. The Department of Environmental Protection has improved a series of trails, begun trail erosion control measures, and installed step-assists on steep grades. To preserve it as a natural area, smoking is not permitted. Animal or geological specimens are not to be touched, and camping and picnicking are forbidden.

DIRECTIONS: Route 206 north. Look for Stokes State Forest office sign on the right. Information, maps, and specific directions are available there.

PART II

MAN-MADE WONDERS

15

Atlantic City Boardwalk

Whenever anyone thinks of the New Jersey shore, Atlantic City, the "Queen of the Ocean," comes first to mind. It is the center of attraction, the shore symbol for nearly half of all visitors to New Jersey resorts.

Every year more than 15 million visitors come to stroll on the famous Boardwalk, to feel the sea breeze, to see where Miss America is crowned every September, and to sunbathe on the white, sandy beaches.

The possibility of Absecon Island as a summer resort was first recognized by Jonathan Pitney, who settled there in 1820 to practice medicine. It remained a germ of an idea until three decades later, when he was the leader of a group that planned Atlantic City and persuaded the Camden and Atlantic Railroad to route its trains to the village.

The first boardwalk was constructed in 1870 because of complaints from railroads and hotels about visitors tracking sand onto their premises. The walk, secured to posts a foot above the sand, was made in 12-foot sections. It could be dismantled easily before the winter.

In 1880 a second and wider boardwalk was built. Four years later the third walk was constructed. This was a permanent structure, four feet above the sand, with an arched overpass at every street to allow horses and buggies to pass under. After the 1889 hurricane, a fourth boardwalk was built, 24 feet wide and ten feet above the sand.

The present boardwalk, built of steel and concrete with pine-plank flooring, is 60 feet wide and five miles long. It takes more than 20 miles of new plank each year to keep it in repair.

To attract crowds, the first Alantic City Easter Parade was held in 1876. Since then the Boardwalk has become known worldwide. The crowds have never stopped coming. A few years later the first of the amusement piers extending into the sea from the Boardwalk was constructed. The most famous and the longest is the Steel Pier at Virginia Avenue. The main attractions there are the roller coaster, the carousel ride, thrill rides, games of chance, disco dancing, a water show with Acapulco cliff divers, and two diving horses.

The Million Dollar Pier at Arkansas Avenue was so-named by the builder, the late Captain John L. Young, because of construction costs. Captain Young's house on the pier had the distinguished address of No. 1 Atlantic Ocean.

The Steeplechase Pier at Pennsylvania Avenue features rides and games for children and adults. The Central Pier has a miniature golf course, a giant slide, and revolving rides.

The Garden Pier at the Boardwalk and New Jersey Avenue is owned by the city and used as a civic center for cultural events, art exhibits, and concerts.

The Boardwalk sights are as free as the salt air, and one can view them all by strolling, bicycling (permitted before 9 a.m.), as a tram-ride passenger, or from a rolling chair.

In the summer of 1978, legalized gambling in Atlantic City was permitted, and four casinos, the first on the East Coast, have opened to an enthusiastic response. Hotels line the Boardwalk and extend inland for several blocks.

Atlantic City is a community in transition. The shiny casinos thrive as visitors pour an average of $1.5 million a day into the gambling halls. But just two blocks west of the Boardwalk there are vacant stores and the streets appear tired and forlorn.

Business, on the whole, is better but not what everybody thought it would be.

The casinos have created 11,000 new jobs for the city's 43,000 residents. With the construction of new casinos on the drawing boards, the city's tax base should quadruple.

The shiny casinos have brought hope for a brighter tomorrow to the aging city by the sea.

Another Atlantic City attraction is its street names. They have become known to millions because of the Monopoly game developed by Charles B. Darrow in 1930.

Convention Hall, on the Boardwalk at Mississippi Avenue, is one of the largest convention centers in the world, seating 41,000. It was big enough to hold the 1964 Democratic National Convention. The organ in Convention Hall, with 32,000 stops, is the world's largest.

Atlantic City Boardwalk
(Atlantic City Press Bureau)

INFORMATION: Atlantic City Convention & Visitors Bureau, 16 Central Pier, Atlantic City, NJ 08401. (609) 345-3305. Visitors' Hot Line, (609) 348-7052.

DIRECTIONS: From North or South, take the Garden State Parkway, Exits 36, 38, 40. From the Philadelphia area take U.S. Route 42 to U.S. 322 to U.S. Route 40/322, U.S. 30 or Atlantic City Expressway (toll road). Frequent bus service is also available from both New York and Philadelphia.

16

ℰdison's
ℰlectric Light Bulb

Thomas A. Edison's accomplishments are many, but his most important contribution was lighting up the world.

Edison, who is considered the country's greatest inventor, invented the phonograph and the motion picture camera, among numerous other devices, but he is best known for making an electric light suitable for everyday use.

Edison and his aides were dedicated to finding a practical system of electric lighting. He did not invent the incandescent lamp nor did he invent electric power. His goal was to make the electric light "so cheap that only the rich will be able to burn candles."

The key to the practical use of electricity was the lamp, and the key to the lamp was finding a long-lasting and inexpensive filament.

He experimented with pieces of cotton thread which he had prepared by carefully burning them into carbon filaments.

After many false starts, he found that cotton filament would glow brightly. It continued to burn for 40 hours through two dark nights. The successful test in 1879 took place in Edison's laboratory in Menlo Park, a section of Edison Township. Visitors to Menlo Park marveled at the lamps that burned brightly both outside and inside the laboratory.

The next step in making electricity available to everyone was a system to transmit the current from generators to homes and businesses.

Edison's plan was to install electric lighting powered from central generating stations; the first one to be located in a half-mile-square area of lower Manhattan. The area included the headquarters of banks and offices of investors whose support Edison needed.

In February, 1881, Edison wrote at Menlo Park, "my work here is done, my light is perfected. I'm going into the practical production of it."

Large-scale use of incandescent lights began in September, 1882, when the Edison Company completed the Pearl Street generating station in New York.

Edison, who had earlier worked in Newark for six years, moved to West Orange in 1886 after the death of his first wife. Later he married Mina Miller, and they made their home at Glenmont, a 23-room brick house in the Llewelyn Park section of West Orange, where he spent the last 44 years of his life. Not far away he built a new and much larger laboratory.

Edison was a complex man about whom we are only now starting to learn more. His varied activities defy quick summary. He was partly deaf, poorly coordinated, with little formal education, but he held 1,093 patents—more than any other individual. By the age of 31, he was well established as a full-time inventor.

One of his habits was to put everything in writing. More than two million pages of memos, letters, laboratory reports, and notebook drawings are now being prepared for publication in a project that will take some 20 years to complete.

The "Wizard of Menlo Park," as Edison has come to be known, was often quoted as saying that "Genius is one

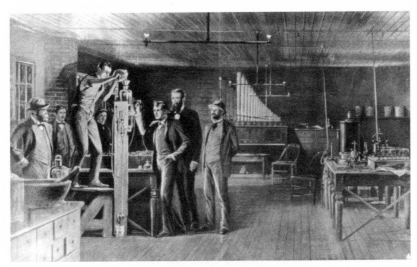

The Edison Laboratory, Menlo Park, N.J., the eve of
"The Birth of a Great Invention"
*(U.S. Department of the Interior, National Park Service,
Edison National Historic Site.)*

percent inspiration and ninety-nine percent perspiration."

Edison died on October 18, 1931. New Jersey had been his home and workshop for 61 years.

INFORMATION: (For Edison Laboratory and Glenmont) Edison National Historic Site, Main St. and Lakeside Ave., West Orange, NJ 07052. (201) 736-5050. Continous guided tours of the laboratory from 9:30 a.m. to 3:30 p.m. daily except Thanksgiving, Christmas, and New Year's Day. The Edison residence, Glenmont, is open for guided tours from noon to 4 p.m., Wednesday through Sunday except holidays. Admission, fifty cents. Those under 16 and over 62 admitted free.

(For Edison Historical Site and Tower) Edison, NJ 08817. (201) 549-3299. Museum is open Tuesday through Saturday from 10 a.m. to noon and 1 p.m. to 5 p.m.; Sunday from 1 p.m. to 5 p.m. Contains displays of Edison's accomplishments from 1876-1886. Admission is twenty-five cents. The Tower, a 131-foot memorial, is on the site of the original laboratory. The laboratory itself and much of Edison's equipment, were moved to Dearborn, Michigan, by Edison's close friend, Henry Ford.

DIRECTIONS: (For Edison Laboratory and Glenmont) From the North or South take the Garden State Parkway, Exit 145, to Interstate 280 west to the Oranges to Exit 10, then right on Northfield Rd., left on Main St., past two lights to the laboratory. From western New Jersey take Interstate 280 east to the Oranges to Exit 9, then left on Mt. Pleasant Ave., left on Main St., past one light to the laboratory.

(For Edison Historical Site and Tower) Garden State Parkway, Exit 131, to Route 27 south.

17

George Washington Bridge

From the center of the majestic George Washington Bridge you are higher than a 20-story building, and you can see miles of New Jersey and Manhattan, as well as the Hudson River vanishing to a pinpoint upstream and flowing into the sea to the south. You are in the middle of a major engineering feat which, when constructed, was the longest suspension bridge in the world.

When the 3500-foot span across the Hudson was opened to vehicular traffic on October 25, 1931, between New Jersey and New York, it was considered an engineering triumph. It became so heavily traveled that a second deck was added in 1962.

Steel twin towers, embedded in rock and cement, one on each side of the river, rise 604 feet above the Hudson. The Roebling Company of Trenton spun the 26,474 steel wires that make up each of the four mighty cables that are suspended in pairs from tower to tower and are anchored on both sides of the river. Suspender cables hang vertically from the three-foot diameter main cables. The final phase of building was the section-by-section attachment of steel frames to the suspender cables to support the roadbed. With the meeting of the last two sections midway over the Hudson River, the roadbed was finished.

During the construction there was a great debate over what the bridge should be named. People were invited to submit names, and there were even newspaper contests. Among the suggestions: Gate of Paradise, Bridge of Prosperity, Noble Experiment, Pride of the Nation, Peoples' Bridge, and Bi-State Bridge. Because both sides of the river were sites of Revolutionary War forts—Fort Lee in New Jersey and Fort Washington in Manhattan—both commanded by General Washington, the Port Authority decided to name it the George Washington Bridge.

When the bridge opened there were six lanes. Four and a half million cars crossed during its first year. Today there are 14 lanes, and nearly 80 million cars cross the bridge annually.

At night when lights glisten on its cables the bridge is a magical sight. On a mild, clear day a walk across the bridge from Fort Lee to Manhattan, slightly less than a mile, is a memorable experience.

During national holidays, one of the largest flags in the world flies from the arch of the New Jersey tower.

The bridge, designed by Othmar Ammann, was completed at a cost of $59 million. Today it is the fourth longest suspension bridge in the world.

When the building of the bridge was about to begin, the chairman of the Port Authority remarked, "This bridge, of simple lines, of dignified mein, and of architectural harmony, will be not only one of the wonders of the world, but a thing of enduring beauty."

The bridge was dedicated by governors Morgan F. Larson of New Jersey and Franklin D. Roosevelt of New York.

George Washington Bridge
(The Port Authority of New York and New Jersey)

INFORMATION: The George Washington Bridge, Port Authority of New York and New Jersey, One World Trade Center, New York, NY 10048. (212) 466-7000.

DIRECTIONS: Major roads such as the New Jersey Turnpike (Route 95), the Garden State Parkway, and Routes 1, 9, 46, and 80 lead to the George Washington Bridge. Open 24 hours. Fee for passenger cars, $1.50, paid by eastbound travelers only.

18

Holland Tunnel

Skeptics said it couldn't be done. But Clifford M. Holland knew otherwise. In 1920 he began the greatest engineering feat of the time, a $54 million project to dig the world's first automobile tunnel under a river. Many called it the eighth wonder of the world.

On November 12, 1927, thousands gathered to witness the opening ceremonies of the Holland Tunnel, linking Jersey City and lower Manhattan under the Hudson River. New Jersey Governor A. Harry Moore and Mayor Frank Hague of Jersey City represented New Jersey, and Governor Al Smith and Mayor Jimmy Walker represented New York. From late in the afternoon until midnight the tunnel was turned over to pedestrians, and more than 20,000 celebrated by walking through it. Then it was closed to pedestrians forever. At 12:01 a.m. November 13, the first automobile rolled through the tunnel, making the trip in eight minutes.

Holland was the tunnel's chief engineer. He supervised the entire construction and designed the twin, 1¾-mile tunnel tubes.

He devised the ventilating system that changes the air every

90 seconds to eliminate accumulations of poisonous fumes from engine exhausts.

Work on the trans-Hudson tunnel began at both ends simultaneously. Each end had its own crew of tunnel-construction workers called "sandhogs." Each crew worked its way towards the other, 90 feet below the river's surface, at the rate of 15 feet a day.

Holland, overworked and exhausted at the age of 41, died October 27, 1924, just one day before the north tube was "holed" through.

The Holland Tunnel pioneered a new era of commerce and transportation between New Jersey and New York and was an example for the construction of other tunnels around the world.

It connects Canal Street in Manhattan with 12th and 14th Streets in Jersey City. Since 1930 the Holland Tunnel has been owned and operated by the Port Authority of New York and New Jersey.

The Holland Tunnel operates around the clock. It requires a staff of 250, including police, toll collectors, maintenance employees, and operations agents.

In 1928, its first year of operation, more than eight million vehicles passed through the tunnel. Today, more than 20 million make the trip annually.

A plaque and bust of Clifford Holland can be found at the New York entrance to the tunnel. The plaque, unveiled in 1977 to mark the tunnel's 50th year, reads: "To commemorate the 50th anniversary of the opening of the Holland Tunnel, the underground highway which joins a continent to a city. He builded better than he knew."

The highlight of the drive through the tunnel in either direction is the marker on the wall under the Hudson that tells when one leaves one state and goes into the other.

Holland Tunnel Dedication Ceremonies, 1927
(Newark Public Library Photo)

Holland Tunnel
(The Port Authority of New York and New Jersey)

INFORMATION: Port Authority of New York and New Jersey, One World Trade Center, New York, NY 10048. (212) 466-7777. The fee for passenger cars is $1.50, paid by eastbound vehicles only.

DIRECTIONS: All major New Jersey roads have well-marked connections leading to the Holland Tunnel.

19

Lucy, the Margate Elephant

Lucy, the Margate Elephant, is one of the world's most whimsical "white elephants." She is now a national historic landmark.

She has been attracting attention since she was built and patented in 1881, by James V. Lafferty to promote sales of his seaside properties.

Lucy weighs 90 tons, is 65 feet high with a canopied seat called a "howdah" on top, and has spiral stairs in her rear legs. Every year some 20,000 visitors climb up in her for a view of the sea and coastline from the howdah which is as high as a six-story building.

Lucy is sculptured of nearly a million pieces of wood and covered with a tin skin. When she was built she amazed seaside tourists with her bulk: 17-foot ears, 22-foot tusks, and a trunk 26 feet long.

For 90 years Lucy has been admired by children and has been a source of amusement for adults and, occasionally, a sobering influence. There is a tale that sailors on ships in the Atlantic are said to have given up rum abruptly after one sight of Lucy towering on the beach, gazing out to sea at them.

Lucy, the Margate Elephant, is an architectural folly—a unique, important part of Americana dating to the Victorian era when craftsmen hand-fashioned ornate buildings.

She is the only one surviving of three elephants built by Lafferty. A fire in 1896 claimed the Coney Island elephant, and Cape May demolished one in 1900.

Lucy has been a private residence, part of a hotel, a restaurant, an office, a summer beach cottage, and a tavern. Lucy's fortunes began to decline after World War II, and by the 1960s she was closed to the public because she had so deteriorated.

Rotting away and facing demolition, Lucy was saved through the efforts of a "Save Lucy" committee. She was moved in 1970 to public park land, and restoration was begun in 1973.

The committee raised $62,000 locally to qualify for a matching grant from the United States Department of Housing and Urban Development. The group was successful in obtaining $30,000 more from the agency for the restoration project. The extra money came when lovable Lucy was officially declared a national historic landmark, the highest honor and recognition in America that can officially be accorded a structure of merit. Lucy has always had lots of friends and supporters, many of whom swarmed to Washington wearing "Save Lucy" buttons, helping Lucy receive landmark status.

Lucy, the Margate Elephant
(W. Earle Hawkins)

INFORMATION: Lucy, the Margate Elephant, 9200 Atlantic Ave., Margate, NJ 08402. (609) 823-6473 or (609) 822-0424. Weekends only: Memorial Day weekend through June 20 and Labor Day through October, 10 a.m. to 4:30 p.m. Daily: June 21 through Labor Day, 10 a.m. to 4:30 p.m.

DIRECTIONS: From northern New Jersey, take the Garden State Parkway, south, to Exit 36. Route 563 south to Margate.

20

Meadowlands: New Jersey Sports Complex

The Meadowlands sports and entertainment center rises unexpectedly from the swamplands in the heart of industrial northeast New Jersey. The land, valuable because of its location but previously considered useless because of its swampy soil structure, now attracts millions of sports fans to its three multipurpose structures silhouetted against Bergen County urban development and the Manhattan skyline. It is the home of the Giants football team and the Cosmos soccer team, as well as the scene of thoroughbred racing, concerts, and special events.

The initial phase of the sports complex, which its developers, the New Jersey Sports and Exposition Authority, called the state's finest man-made asset, opened in 1976 with the first professional football game in Giants Stadium and harness racing on the Meadowlands Racetrack. Thoroughbred racing began at the track the following year.

In 1981, the current phase, the Meadowlands Arena—accomodating a wide range of indoor sports—will be opened.

Giants Stadium is designed especially, but not exclusively, for football, with every seat offering an unobstructed view. The playing surface accommodates an international-size soccer field and is exceptionally suited for other sports such as tennis and lacrosse, as well as events such as concerts, rodeos, circuses, and outdoor conventions. Since the stadium opened every home game of the Giants has been sold out in advance, and Pele, who attracted record crowds whenever he appeared there, helped the Cosmos soccer team to its present popularity.

The Meadowlands racetrack is equipped for both daytime and nighttime thoroughbred and harness racing. The one-mile track is convertible from a limestone surface for harness racing to a loam surface for flat racing. There is also a 7/8-mile turf track for thoroughbred races. The six-level racetrack grandstand is completely enclosed and is climate-controlled. As many as 35,000 spectators can be accommodated, and there are stables for 1,700 horses.

When the $70 million Meadowlands Arena opens it will seat up to 21,000 and will have parking for 4,000 cars on the 70-acre site. It is designed for multiple usage—sports, pageants, expositions, conventions, and trade shows. It will become the home court for the New Jersey Nets basketball team. There are also discussions about a major league hockey franchise locating here.

Giants Stadium is getting increased use from college teams. The racetrack has broken all attendance records and has attracted such world-famous races as the Hambletonian.

The Meadowlands is the most successful publicly-owned sports and exposition facility in the country.

INFORMATION: New Jersey Sports & Exposition Authority, 50 Route 20, East Rutherford, NJ 07073. (201) 935-8500.

DIRECTIONS: Located on Route 3 between the Garden State Parkway and the Lincoln Tunnel. Take Route 3, the New Jersey Turnpike Exit 16W, Route 17, or Route 20

Meadlowlands Sports Complex
(New Jersey Sports & Exposition Authority)

Meadlowlands Sports Complex
(Newark Public Library Photo)

and follow the Sports Complex signs. It is four miles west of the Lincoln Tunnel, and eight miles from the George Washington Bridge.

21

Twin Lights
Navesink Lighthouse

Perched in a strategic location to overlook both the bay and the ocean, the Twin Lights of Navesink keep a silent vigil over the Highlands and the pounding surf below. This twin-tower lighthouse easily can be considered a New Jersey wonder because of its importance in early navigation and communications.

The Twin Lights provide an exceptional view of Sandy Hook, New York Harbor, and the Atlantic Ocean.

The towers, 73 feet high, 254 feet above sea level, and connected by a fortress-like brick and stone structure, are not identical twins, however. The south tower is square, and the north one is octagonal.

The Highlands had been a signal station since the early days of shipping. Once lookouts with spyglasses watched from the Highlands to see far-off ships. Later the twin lighthouse warned ship captains of the dangerous coastline, preventing many sea tragedies. The original station was built in 1828 on Beacon Hill, 250 feet above sea level. It was flawed by faulty workmanship and materials, however, and was replaced by the Twin Lights in 1862.

In 1841, the first Fresnel long-range lens in this country was imported from France and installed in one of the towers. This lens made an improvement in the light, which made Twin Lights famous; some said the lights could be seen 40 miles at sea. It's a light sailors still talk about.

In 1898, the first electric arc lamp used in a lighthouse was installed in the south tower. In September 1899, Guglielmo Marconi used the lighthouse to demonstrate his invention, the wireless telegraph, by communicating with a vessel at sea.

The twin lights also cast a warm glow on later history. During World War II, radar experiments for locating ships were carried on at Twin Lights. Ironically, success of ship radar led to the decommissioning of the lighthouse in 1949 by the federal government. Today only a blinker light shines as a guide to local boat traffic.

The borough of Highlands reached agreement with the General Services Administration in 1954 to restore and maintain the buildings and grounds.

In 1960 the state accepted responsibility for maintenance of the buildings, and Twin Lights became an official state historic site.

An historical and maritime museum was established by the Twin Lights Historical Society, and is now in full operation. The museum contains a collection of memorabilia and photographs of the area, relating to lighthouses, the United States Lifesaving Service, boating and fishing industries of the Jersey shore, and steamboats. It includes the first lifesaving station built on Sandy Hook in 1849. There are logs of several ships, navigational instruments, steamship engines, and other artifacts. The 1898 Fresnel lens is now on exhibit in the museum.

Twin Lights
(Paul J. Taylor, Bureau of Parks)

INFORMATION: The Navesink Twin Lights, Route 36, Highlands, NJ 07732. Cheesequake State Park Office, (201) 566-2161. The museum is open to visitors daily except Monday from Memorial Day through Labor Day, 9 a.m. to 5 p.m. year round.

DIRECTIONS: From Northern New Jersey, take the Garden State Parkway to Exit 117. Take Route 36 and turn immediately before the Highlands Bridge over the river. Follow the black and white signs to the Lighthouse.

22

Branch Brook Park Cherry Blossoms

It's pretty pink and white as far as the eye can see. It's the celebration of spring in Newark's Branch Brook Park, and the beauty of the cherry blossoms attracts more than one-half million visitors annually.

During the last two weeks in April, more than 2,000 Oriental cherry trees, in eleven varieties, explode into color with millions of pink and white flowers.

The annual display is larger than the one in Washington, D.C. in numbers, varieties, and masses of plantings.

The first 180 trees were planted in the park in 1928 around the tennis courts near Heller Parkway. These were part of a group of 2,050 trees purchased with funds donated by Mrs. Felix Fuld, a member of the Bamberger family. The bulk of the remaining trees was planted in Branch Brook extension in 1933, with the first full flowering occurring four years later.

Many weeping varieties of trees border Second River where their beauty is reflected in the sunlit stream.

The blossoms open more or less at once, last for a couple of weeks, and then swiftly fade.

The cherry trees are divided into two groups. The single blossoms, with five petals each, bloom about April 15-20. The Higan Cherry, the earliest to bloom, comes in two varieties. One variety grows from 15 to 18 feet wide and high and has large blossoms of brilliant pink. The other variety is a weeping variety, which produces smaller blossoms. The Yoshino Cherry has large pink petals that fade to white, and the Sargentis Cherry's deep pink leaves open to purple and turn to green.

The double blossoms, multiples of five petals, bloom ten to fourteen days after the single blossoms.

Varieties include the Kwanzan Cherry, pink with frills at the tips of petals; Shirotae Cherry, like the Kwanzan but with a wider petal spread; Fugenzo, like the Kwanzan, but a slower grower; Amanogawa Cherry, a tall, narrow shape, light pink; Gyoiko Cherry, a slower grower with greenish or yellowish blossoms; and the Shirofugen Cherry, deep pink that fades to white as a mature plant.

The Essex County Department of Parks, Recreation, and Cultural Affairs and its horticulture staff provide the maintenance of the trees. Careful pruning occurs in March. Trees are sprayed in March, with a miscible oil, and in June, with other insecticides, to protect them against chewing insects.

The trees have a life span of only 35 to 40 years, and the grafting of new plants from the first collection began as early as 1929.

Mrs. Fuld provided a trust fund for the maintenance and replacement of the trees. Donations of trees continue through grants from corporations and individuals.

The cherry blossoms in Branch Brook Park offer beauty and serenity in the midst of the urban environment of Newark, and the annual Newark Cherry Blossom Festival is also a showcase of cultural events.

Branch Brook Park, Cherry Blossoms
(Collection of the Newark Museum)

INFORMATION: Essex County Department of Parks, Recreation, and Cultural Affairs Office, 115 Clifton Ave., Newark, NJ 07104. (201) 482-6400.

DIRECTIONS: North on the Garden State Parkway to Exit 145. Route 280 east to the Newark exit. Left at exit light to Park Ave. Right on Park Ave. and left into Branch Brook Park. By mass transit from Newark's Pennsylvania Station or Public Service Terminal, take city subway to the end of the line. The park is a short distance away.

23

Bell Laboratories, Inc., Murray Hill

Bell Laboratories at Murray Hill is the headquarters of the research and development unit of the Bell System. Bell Labs is one of the world's great research facilities and the source of most of the world's telecommunications technology for the past half century.

Seven Bell Labs scientists have received Nobel prizes including one for the discovery of the transistor, which spawned the age of electronics, computers, and satellites. Bell Labs scientists and engineers have been granted more than one patent every working day since Bell Laboratories was established in 1925.

Other significant contributions made there are the solar cell, laser, maser, discovery of wave nature of matter, radio astronomy, hi-fidelity recording, Picturephone, long-distance television transmission, and satellite communications.

More than 4,100 employees work here on 215 acres.

At Murray Hill two days before Christmas in 1947, scientists invented the transistor, now a common component in everyday use. It would, among other things, make instant replay possible, as well as intercontinental television, computers, and miniature radios.

The three scientists who invented the transistor were John Bardeen, Walter Brattain, and William Shockley.

The transistor was used first to improve telephone service. The transistor radio was marketed in 1954. Later it was used in space exploration and satellite communication.

"Mission: Communications," the Bell Labs lobby exhibit, provides an audio-visual review of landmark scientific discoveries and inventions, mixed with a mind-stretching look into the future of electronic telecommunications.

Behind the elaborate system of relays and switches that make fast, high-quality, low-cost telephone service possible is an intriguing history of scientific advances. More than fifty years of technical achievement come to life in the exhibit, where visitors can see:

1. a replica of Alexander Graham Bell's first "liquid" telephone (1876)
2. the first long distance television system (1927)
3. America's first talking pictures (1927). Bell Labs designed the system for synchronizing film dialogue on a disk used in the production of the first sound movie, "The Jazz Singer."
4. the high speed motion picture camera (1934)
5. the first transistor (1947), that paved the way for today's solid-state electronics industry
6. the solar cell (1954), the first practical device to convert the sun's energy into usable electricity— found aboard U.S. spacecraft
7. one of the six original Telstar communications satellites (1962)

Here glimpses into the future of telecommunications include a television signal sent over a single, hair-thin lightguide and a presentation of various experimental components for lightwave communications systems. Visitors will also learn about the work of the engineers in the field of integrated circuits, about light-emitting diodes, and about the use of simulated crystals and magnetic bubbles.

Exhibit highlights include a demonstration of the Picturephone system, the innovation that makes it possible for callers to see the person with whom they are talking on a television screen. Guests will begin to realize that the age of "Star Wars" may not be far off when they are addressed by a computer simulating a human voice.

Bell Laboratories, Murray Hill
(Bell Laboratories, Inc.)

INFORMATION: Bell Laboratories, 600 Mountain Ave., Murray Hill, NJ 07974. (201) 582-3000. The exhibit is open to the public Saturdays and Sundays from 1 p.m. to 5 p.m. in the east wing of the pyramid-like main building. Group tours during the week by appointment.

DIRECTIONS: From Route 22 west, turn west at the Scotch Plains exit. Turn right to Union Ave. and right onto Diamond Hill Rd. to the second traffic light. Turn right onto Mountain Ave. Bell Labs is four-tenths of a mile on the right.

24

Cape May

Cape May is Victorian charm on the southern tip of the New Jersey shore. A town of seaside pleasures and landmark buildings, Cape May is an American resort classic.

In 1976, because of its large concentration of Victorian structures, it was designated a national historic landmark. The fact is that nearly all the Victorian buildings in Cape May are private properties.

Walking down Cape May streets, a visitor can delight in architectural details such as lattices, scrolls, and gingerbread that decorate the eaves, porches, and windows of so many of the homes. The motifs include leaves, vines, and even waves breaking upside down.

The whaling industry provided the economy of eighteenth century Cape May. About 60 years later businessmen hit on the idea of attracting tourists to Cape May to enjoy sea breezes and ocean bathing.

It sometimes took Philadelphians four days to make the trip by stagecoach. They were joined by rich Southerners, bringing gold for gambling, and arriving in June with their entourages of servants to settle in for the summer.

Instead of hotel life, some wanted to own their cottages, and they acquired some of the best architects to design them.

Destroyed by fire in the late 1800s, Cape May has been re-built with charm and a quiet dignity that can be seen in more than 250 Victorian buildings.

The wide front porches, the gingerbread, and the widow's walks are delights of Cape May. All of the architectural treasures add to the enjoyment of white beaches.

In some guest houses there are high ceilings, fussy fur-nishings, and long lace curtains. Tea and cookies are served on the side verandas.

Cape May has one of the largest collections of late nine-teenth century frame buildings in the United States. It contains more than 600 summer houses, old hotels, and commerical structures. It is a kind of textbook of American taste in buildings.

Some famous visitors were Henry Clay, who came in the hot August of 1847, Abraham Lincoln in 1849, Franklin Pierce in 1855, James Buchanan in 1858, Ulysses S. Grant in 1873, Chester A. Arthur in 1883, and Benjamin Harrison in 1889.

The Mt. Vernon Hotel, the largest in the world when con-structed in 1853, burned in 1856.

The traditional styles found in Cape May include Greek Revival, Gothic, Queen Anne, Italianate, Eastlake, and Mansard.

Cape May is charm, whimsical romance, and nostalgia. From the unique stick-style shingle of Dr. Emlen Physick's house to the delightful Pink House, with the most ornamented porch in the city, Cape May is a showcase of the late Victorian period of architecture.

Other delights of Cape May send visitors searching for Cape May "diamonds," clear silicate pebbles found on the beach, that resemble diamonds when cut and polished.

At Cape May Point, a sunken concrete ship, the "Atlantis," is a memorable attraction. An experimental ship built of concrete during World War I, it has gradually sunk deeper and

Cape May: Emlen Physick House
(City of Cape May, Department of Public Relations & Recreations)

deeper in the sand since it was blown aground in a storm in 1926.

INFORMATION: Public Relations Department, City of Cape May, NJ 08204. (609) 884-8411. Victorian Mall Information Booth (609) 884-0012. Walking tours of Victorian highlights, the annual house tour in July, sponsored by the Cape May County Art League, the Cape May Candlelight Tour in December, an old-fashioned trolley, a Victorian Mall, and the Cape May-Lewes Ferry. Fee for ferry is $8.00 for cars, $2.00 for passengers. For the ferry schedule, write P.O. Box 827, Cape May, NJ 08204.

DIRECTIONS: About 140 miles from New York, 90 miles from Philadelphia, accessible by Route 9 or Ocean Drive and the Garden State Parkway.

Cape May: Pink House
(City of Cape May, Department of Public Relations & Recreations)

25

The Newark-Elizabeth Transportation Complex

The area along the shoreline of Newark Bay is the transportation hub of the East. Its purpose is to move people and things in and out of America quickly and efficiently. Whether by plane, train, ship, or truck, the port's network of air and sea lanes, rail lines, and superhighway links gets the job done.

Every month more than 750,000 people arrive at or depart from Newark International Airport to and from cities all over America and the world. Every month a million tons of cargo are handled in bustling Ports Newark and Elizabeth.

Thousands of ships are docked every year in the channels of Ports Newark and Elizabeth, called "America's Container Capital," because 70 percent of the cargo coming and going is in standardized containers that can be loaded quickly by huge cranes onto ships, on trucks, or on flat cars especially designed to transport them.

The channel in Elizabeth is 9,000 feet long, in Newark, 7,000 feet. Both are more than 600 feet wide, and combined they have more than 40,000 feet of berthing space.

Giant cargo-distribution buildings, warehouses, and other

miscellaneous service structures dot the 2,000 acres of the ports. Huge cranes that form a skyline of their own hoist the containers on and off the ships, rail flatcars, and trucks.

The cargo centers contain the wealth of the world: fruit, hides, lumber, coffee, metal. There are exotic things from exotic lands, and made-in-America tools, tractors, and machinery—all to be loaded for shipment to distant ports. The outdoor fields glisten with the rainbow of colors from acres of imported cars awaiting delivery to car dealers all over America.

The Port Authority of New York and New Jersey has operated Port Newark since 1948, and Port Elizabeth since 1958. It has spent more than $400 million in developing them into the busiest deep-sea port in the world.

Just across the New Jersey Turnpike from Port Newark is Newark International Airport, one of the busiest airports in the East.

The airport, which accomodates 16 airlines and serves more than eight million passengers a year, was begun as a 68-acre venture in 1928, by the city of Newark. The $1,750,000 project included a 1600-foot asphalt runway, the first hard-surface strip on any commercial airport in the country. Its 120-foot square hangar was capable of housing 25 aircraft.

The airport was designated the New York metropolitan airmail terminus in 1929, the same year that scheduled passenger service began with flights conducted by four airlines. By the fall of 1930, Newark International Airport was the busiest in the world, and the same fall the first all-air passenger service to the West Coast was inaugurated. The flight took 36 hours.

Captain Eddie Rickenbacker set a new passenger transport record from Los Angeles to Newark, of thirteen hours and two minutes in 1934. A year later Amelia Earhart flew non-stop from Mexico City to Newark in 14 hours and nine minutes. In 1936, Howard Hughes set a new West-to-East Coast record when he landed at Newark nine hours and 26 minutes after taking off in Burbank, California.

The Army Air Corps operated Newark International Airport during World War II, when its runways and other facilities were expanded, and by the War's end, the airport represented a capital investment of more than $20 million.

In 1948, the city of Newark leased the airport to the Port Authority (now the Port Authority of New York and New Jersey) which began a development program that increased the airport area from 1,400 acres to 2,300 acres.

In 1952, a new instrument runway was constructed at a cost of $9 million, and a year later a passenger terminal was completed for $8.5 million.

New runways have been built, and other new construction includes the administration building, a new fuel storage-tank farm, new taxiways, roadways, and the passenger terminals currently in use.

In all, the city of Newark has about $8.2 million invested in the international airport, the U.S. Government more than $15 million, and the Port Authority of New York and New Jersey about $405 million.

Newark International Airport
(The Port Authority of New York and New Jersey)

INFORMATION: The Port Authority of New York and New Jersey tours are conducted Monday through Friday, 9:30 a.m. to 3:30 p.m. Tours begin at 260 Transit Street, Newark, and offer visitors a glimpse of activity involving the port, its piers, and container shipping. Call (201) 589-7100 to make arrangements. Group and school tours of Newark International Airport are available through the Port Authority. Call (201) 961-2066.

Port Newark
(Newark Public Library Photo)

DIRECTIONS: From the New Jersey Turnpike north take
Exit 14, marked Newark Airport. Follow signs to Port
Newark and Northside Terminal. Right turn on Marlin St.,
right turn on Distribution St. to the Port's administration
building.
Newark International Airport is accessible from Routes
1 and 9, Route 22, the New Jersey Turnpike (exit 14),
Route 78, as well as from Manhattan via the New Jersey
Turnpike.

26

Trenton
Psychiatric Hospital

Determined that all who were sick, old, weak, or deranged must receive humane treatment, Dorothea Dix of Massachusetts swept through New Jersey in 1843 to survey the state's jails, almshouses, and mental asylums.

Miss Dix worked on behalf of the large and much-neglected group of sufferers, and she exposed a statewide chamber of horrors, revealing scenes of almost incredible sufferings.

She visited every jail and every almshouse. Nothing escaped her eye. She saw chains and straw beds. She found the insane confined to cells pervaded with foul air, and the ill kept in the dark, damp, unfurnished, and unheated quarters.

In Trenton, she called for construction of a state lunatic asylum. She was so effective that legislators reported a month later that they could only repeat what was so effectively said by Miss Dix. This social crusader was articulate and persuasive, a pioneer in social reform. *She* succeeded where committees, commissions, and well-meaning reports had failed. She convinced lawmakers that they must spend $150,000 for a new asylum and that it must be an isolated community with peaceful surroundings and plenty of room.

Her stirring report of appalling conditions in the state was first met with indifference, but Miss Dix continued to press legislators, who voted in April of 1844, for a new mental hospital near Trenton.

Miss Dix herself chose the location for the new hospital, 100 acres north of Trenton, overlooking the Delaware River. It was designed and built with the greatest of care to give form to an important and exciting idea. The building faced the Delaware on the west to take advantage of the sun and breezes. In 1848 it opened its doors with 86 patients. It was the state's first hospital and in Dorothea Dix's heart her "first-born child."

She never forgot New Jersey or the hospital, the first of many she would help to establish. In her long years of traveling she often stopped at Trenton to visit and she always sent books and plants to the patients.

She was 80 years old and touring some of the hospitals she had founded when she became ill, but she continued to Trenton to regain her strength. The hospital trustees offered her a small apartment under the eaves, where she spent the last six years of her life under the care of the hospital staff until her death in 1887.

There are about 900 patients at the Trenton Psychiatric Hospital today. The hospital diagnoses and treats mentally-ill patients from Mercer, Hunterdon, Warren, Somerset, Hudson, and a portion of Essex counties, as well as providing custodial treatment for those patients adjudged criminally insane from all parts of the state.

The hospital has been added to ever since its construction in 1848, the latest addition being a children's and adolescent's center, built in the late 1970s.

Today Trenton Psychiatric Hospital offers, among other services, group therapy, 24-hour hospital care, contacts with schools of nursing and social work, and a residency program for psychiatrists. Patient-care programs are run by teams of

Trenton Psychiatric Hospital
(Special Collection, Rutgers University Library)

medical professionals, and transitional-living homes help to prepare patients for re-entering the community.

INFORMATION: Trenton Psychiatric Hospital, Sullivan Way, P.O. Box 7500 Trenton, NJ 08628. (609) 396-8261. An Awareness Day is held in March. Tours are available by appointment through the volunteer service department.

DIRECTIONS: From Route 31 south, turn right to Ewingville Rd., right to Lower Ferry Rd., and left to Sullivan Way. From downtown Trenton take Route 29 north across the Delaware and Raritan Canal bridge to Sullivan Way.

27

Society for Establishing Useful Manufactures

The Society for Establishing Useful Manufactures, popularly known as S.U.M., was established through the efforts of Alexander Hamilton in 1791. The goal of S.U.M. was to build a carefully-planned industrial community using the Great Falls of the Passaic River as its energy source. S.U.M. would give birth to the city of Paterson, which, over the course of its history, would spawn industries in textiles, locomotives, and aircraft. Justifiably, it may be called the "cradle of American industry."

On July 10, 1778, less than two weeks after the Battle of Monmouth, General George Washington, Colonel Alexander Hamilton, and other Revolutionary War leaders paused for a brief rest overlooking the Great Falls. Thirteen years later, Secretary of the Treasury Hamilton proposed that the new federal government should develop home industries as a means of strengthening our new nation. While the founding fathers did not agree to federal funding for the proposal, Hamilton managed to secure the capital necessary for the project from some wealthy businessmen. The ideal location for such an industrial complex, argued Hamilton, would be in the area of the Great

Falls. On November 22, 1791, the New Jersey Legislature passed, and Governor William Paterson signed, the charter that gave legal existence and generous fringe benefits to S.U.M.

French architect Pierre L'Enfant was hired to draw up plans for this new industrial community, named in honor of Governor Paterson. L'Enfant's plans, which included a raceway system, were considered too elaborate and expensive, and he was dismissed.

Succeeding L'Enfant was Peter Colt, who built Paterson's first cotton mill. Colt successfully utilized the water above the falls by diverting the powerful current into a series of canals, or raceways that guided the water rapidly downhill, providing power for the mills, and eventually emptying the water into the Passaic River below the falls.

During the first few years of its existence the S.U.M. complex did not realize its goals, or its profits. In 1796 it suspended operations and became a "ghost town."

After the War of 1812, the Industrial Revolution would come to the United States and, within a century, this country would lead the world as the foremost industrial giant. The story of industrial Paterson is the story of industrial America.

No one is more responsible for the S.U.M. renaissance than Roswell Colt. While he was the head of the S.U.M. corporation during the first half of the nineteenth century, cotton mills began to flourish, and prime land was sold to promising entrepreneurs. Roswell's cousin, Samuel Colt, founded the Patent Arms Company, which manufactured "the gun that won the West." It was Sam's brother Chris who established S.U.M.'s first silk mill.

No one mode of transportation contributed more to the growth of our country than the railroad. In 1837 Thomas Rogers tested his first locomotive, the "Sandusky," at his factory in Paterson, and by 1880 Paterson was producing 80 percent of the locomotives built in this country. With the advent of the twentieth century, came another mode of transportation, the airplane. In 1927 it was the Wright Aeronautical Company of Paterson that built the engine to propel "The Spirit of St. Louis" and its "Lone Eagle" pilot, Charles Lindbergh, across the Atlantic.

Another Paterson success story unfolded in the silk industry. From the 1840s to the 1940s, Paterson would reign as "The Silk City." John Ryle, an Englishman, later known as the "Father of the silk industry in Paterson," brought his expertise to S.U.M. in the 1840s, and by the turn of the century nearly 300 silk factories were flourishing. Paterson's supremacy in the silk industry was brought to an end both by the development of synthetic fibers such as rayon and nylon and by war with Japan, our chief source of raw silk.

Recently the 119-acre Great Falls/S.U.M. Historic District received a large federal grant for restoring the 49 mills still standing.

During the 1976 bicentennial celebrations, President Gerald R. Ford traveled to Paterson to designate the district as an official national historic landmark, the only industrial district in the United States so honored. In doing so, President Ford acknowledged that Paterson was truly the "cradle of American industry."

S.U.M. Historic District
(Great Falls Development Corporation)

INFORMATION: S.U.M. Historic District, 80 McBride Ave., Paterson, NJ 07501. (201) 881-3896. May through September, tours daily from 9 a.m. to 4:30 p.m. October through April, tours Monday through Friday, 9 a.m. to 4:30 p.m.

DIRECTIONS: Route 80 west, take Paterson Main St. exit. Two blocks on Main to Oliver, left on Oliver to Spruce. Right on Spruce to McBride Ave. and Haines Overlook Park.
Route 80 east, take Paterson Central Business District exit to Grand St. Left on Grand St. and one block to Spruce St.
Garden State Parkway south, take Interstate 80 exit and follow Route 80 west directions above.
Garden State Parkway north, take Exit 155P, continue 2.4 miles until road ends at Grand St. Follow Route 80 east directions above.

28

Cathedral
of the Sacred Heart

New Jerseyites do not have to travel to London, Paris, or New York to visit an impressive cathedral. The magnificent Cathedral of the Sacred Heart in Newark is the same size as Westminster Abbey in London. Its twin towers are higher than those of Notre Dame in Paris, and it is 33 feet longer than St. Patrick's in New York.

The French Gothic Cathedral of the Sacred Heart is massive, resembling most closely the great cathedral at Rheims, France. Its towers soar 232 feet and are visible from most parts of the city and many of the suburbs. It is the fifth largest cathedral in the United States.

In 1896 a proposal to build a new cathedral was first presented to Bishop Winand M. Wigger of the Diocese of Newark. The project gained support and construction, begun in 1898, was completed a half century later, in 1954.

Members of the congregation contributed their pennies and dollars to help meet the cost of having the cathedral built. The first architect was Jeremiah O'Rourke, who was responsible for the ground floor, side aisles, and the perimeter of the cathedral.

Intermediate architects were William Schickel and Isaac Ditmars. The final architect was Paul C. Reilly, who was responsible for the major part of the work involved.

It was during the Reilly architectural stage that Archibishop Thomas Joseph Walsh was named head of the archdiocese and he vowed to "get the cathedral completed and put into use... no matter what it costs." It was completed October 21, 1954.

Visitors can experience the magnitude of the cathedral as they pass through the huge, heavy, bronze doors.

The highly ornamented narthex screen contains symbolic carvings, sculpture, and cresting. The great transom screens leading to Clifton Avenue represent the Old Testament and those leading to Ridge Street, the New Testament.

The vaulted ceilings are of self-supporting masonry construction, built by the same methods used by master builders of the Gothic cathedrals of France and England.

The cathedral's exterior is faced with Vermont granite, and the interior with Indiana limestone, with white-oak woodwork and floors of Italian marble. Most of the statues are of white marble from Carrara in Italy. Mosaics adorn the 14 altars serving as stations of the cross. The Sanctuary is enhanced by a burnished bronze crucifix with a life-like figure of Christ carved from a block of Portugese rose onyx. There are eight chapels radiating from the ambulatory including the Lady Chapel with its marble altar in the apse. Many of the chapels are dedicated to national saints representing the various groups of immigrants comprising the state's Catholic population.

The windows are the work of Franz Zettler, renowned stained-glass craftsman from Munich, Germany. His achievement can be seen in the three magnificent rose windows. The beautiful gallery rose is the second largest church window in the country and is best viewed in the late afternoon sunlight.

The cathedral offers concerts and recitals on its well-known pipe organ.

Cathedral of the Sacred Heart
(Newark Public Library Photo)

INFORMATION: Cathedral of the Sacred Heart, Clifton, Sixth and Park Aves., Newark, NJ 07104. (201) 484-4600. Saturday evening mass at 5:30 p.m. Sunday services of worship: Mass at 8:00 a.m., 9:45 a.m., 12 a.m. Spanish mass at 10:45. When there are no services, the cathedral is closed. Tours are available each Sunday following the 12:00 mass. Group tours can be arranged at other times by calling the cathedral. Concert information is also available at the cathedral.

DIRECTIONS: From the Garden State Parkway, exit 145, to Route 280 east to the Newark exit. Left at the exit light to Park Ave., right on Park Ave. to Clifton Ave. or Ridge St.

Index